BROKEN
AND MADE
WHOLE

MICKI GREEN

WESTBOW
PRESS®
A DIVISION OF THOMAS NELSON
& ZONDERVAN

Copyright © 2016 Micki Green.

All rights reserved. No part of this book may be used or reproduced by any means, graphic, electronic, or mechanical, including photocopying, recording, taping or by any information storage retrieval system without the written permission of the author except in the case of brief quotations embodied in critical articles and reviews.

Scripture taken from the King James Version of the Bible.

Scriptures taken from the Holy Bible, New International Version®, NIV®. Copyright © 1973, 1978, 1984, 2011 by Biblica, Inc.™ Used by permission of Zondervan. All rights reserved worldwide. www.zondervan.com The "NIV" and "New International Version" are trademarks registered in the United States Patent and Trademark Office by Biblica, Inc.™ All rights reserved.

WestBow Press books may be ordered through booksellers or by contacting:

WestBow Press
A Division of Thomas Nelson & Zondervan
1663 Liberty Drive
Bloomington, IN 47403
www.westbowpress.com
1 (866) 928-1240

Because of the dynamic nature of the Internet, any web addresses or links contained in this book may have changed since publication and may no longer be valid. The views expressed in this work are solely those of the author and do not necessarily reflect the views of the publisher, and the publisher hereby disclaims any responsibility for them.

Any people depicted in stock imagery provided by Thinkstock are models, and such images are being used for illustrative purposes only. Certain stock imagery © Thinkstock.

ISBN: 978-1-5127-4265-7 (sc)
ISBN: 978-1-5127-4264-0 (e)

Library of Congress Control Number: 2016908056

Print information available on the last page.

WestBow Press rev. date: 8/16/2016

Dedicated

to my family and friends
who help me keep my eyes on Jesus

Acknowledgements

My deepest gratitude to
- my husband, Dave for his love and support
- my children for standing by me
- my extended family for encouraging me
- my friends Joanne, Sue, and Beverly
for manuscript preparation
and Dave and Dingamon Teuling for chalk art instruction
- my Pastor Andrew and Eryn for computer and practical help
- my church friends for cheering me on
- my Savior for giving me life and reason to write

CHAPTER 1

Before TV, before electronic games.... there were crayons, baby dolls and imagination!

My older sister was at school and as a four year old, I needed to entertain myself. As my mom stood ironing, I would sit at my little play desk drawing pictures and making up stories about each one to her amusement.

When she finished and put away the ironing board, I would carefully stack my pictures in a pile so that when my daddy came home from work, I could share them with him, once again letting my imagination bring them to life.

As mom moved into the kitchen to prepare supper, I would busy myself caring for my dolls, dressing and undressing them, pretending to feed them and making sure they felt very loved.

Looking back, I can see that from earliest childhood my passion for art and love of motherhood were part of the clay God used to form the vessel of my life.

Life in the 1940s was fairly simple for a little girl, but one thing troubled me. Although my parents faithfully took my sister and me to church and Sunday school each week, often the tranquility of our home was disrupted with arguments between them that sent me sobbing to my bedroom. Why did they argue? Did they love each other? Would one of them leave us? Sometimes I would curl up on my bed with my collection of Sunday school papers. I loved the soft colors of the pictures and stories of Jesus but one in particular brought me comfort during those times. Jesus stood, holding a little lamb in His arms and I pretended that I was that lamb.

I knew that He loved me and that He would never leave me. That image has comforted me throughout my life.

"He tends his flock like a shepherd: He gathers the lambs in his arms and carries them close to his heart" (Isaiah 40:11, NIV).

I realized that Jesus took the punishment for my sin when he died on the cross and I asked him to be my Savior and live in me. I knew the Bible says that Jesus loves children. As they surrounded him,

"... he took them up in his arms,
put his hands upon them and blessed them"
(Mark 10:14, KJV).

Eventually, the front door would slam; the voices would be silent. Knowing my dad had left, I would quietly make my way to my mother's side and peer into her tearful eyes. In her arms, I felt safe and we would go on as if nothing had happened.

Despite the problems between them, they were good parents and wanted the best for us.

Moving from an apartment to a home of our own was one of their goals, so on weekends we would go house hunting. One day we found it - a grey stucco home on a tree-lined street with a big back yard. Seven thousand dollars seemed like a fortune, in 1944 but Dad worked two jobs so that we could have this house, the right place for our family.

Great excitement filled the air! It was moving day! Our small apartment was empty, the moving van had left and we were riding the streetcar to our new home on the far north side of Chicago. In my five-year-old mind, it was a mansion – a two-story house with screened porches, three bedrooms, a big back yard and garage. It needed lots of work but that mattered little to my sister and me. We each had a room of our own! We had no car, so half the garage became a chicken coop and the other half was transformed into a playhouse for me and my sister. A picket fence separated it from the garden, flower boxes graced the windows, and inside the playhouse was everything needed to take care of my dolls. Being four years older, my sister wasn't interested, so it was pretty much my domain. Dad built a swing set under the big elm tree and lots of neighborhood kids played there. Each spring, a box of baby chicks was delivered to our house and the chicken coop came alive. The chicks grew quickly and by fall neighbors placed orders for fresh-dressed fryers. I didn't like the smell of wet feathers as I stood on a stool, watching my mother pull them out but I did like eating the boiled chicken feet sprinkled with salt. Yum!

I loved music and a toy piano stood in the corner of the dining room. It was a miniature spinet style piano with three octaves, so I could practice for my thirty-five cent piano lesson given weekly at school. The teacher pounding on my fingers when I made a mistake was a great incentive to get it right.

When I was old enough, once a week I proudly wore my Girl Scout uniform and enjoyed troop meetings with other girls after school. Moral values were instilled in me-honesty, tolerance, selflessness, along with basic life skills like sewing and cooking which have been useful throughout my life.

My elementary school days were filled with things I loved. Except for the pain caused by my parent's problems, life was good and fairly uneventful with one exception. When I was about 12 years old, my parents were attending a special event. Since my sister planned to be out that evening, for the first time they decided to let me come home with a friend, before they returned. They always took us with them, so I was excited that they trusted me to be "home alone", or at least with my friend.

When we got home we decided to fool around at the piano playing Chopsticks and everything else we could think up that we both knew. Soon my parents and sister came home, my friend left and we trudged upstairs to get ready for bed. Suddenly, my dad ran up the stairs with a baseball bat in his hand. "Stay upstairs!" he shouted as he ran down to call the police. We heard him explain how an intruder had broken into our basement and had tried to use an ax to break the lock on the door leading from the basement to the hallway. The police found no one and before leaving helped my dad secure the basement door where the man broke in. We were all shaken up, realizing that when my friend and I came home, we scared him off before he got into the house.

Five minutes later, we would have met him face to face and only God knows what would have happened. That was the first and last time that my parents allowed me to come home when they weren't there.

As I look back, I see how God protected me and although I was not conscious of His work, He was kneading the clay of my life into a vessel He would use for His purposes.

CHAPTER 2

What could be better than to be a teen in the 1950s? Rock and Roll changed the music world and drove parents crazy. Every kid had to have white buck shoes, penny loafers and of course, girls needed saddle oxfords to wear with their felt circle skirts that were decorated with poodles. (If you don't know what I am talking about, ask your grandparents. They will probably tell you more than you want to hear.) My parents were very conservative, so I wasn't allowed to dance, but during lunch period, I watched my friends and gradually came to like this new sound.

High school was very scary for me at first, but before long, I connected with kids and started to enjoy it. I sang in the girls' choir and took an art major which meant two periods a day in the art room. I could lose myself making copper enameled jewelry, creating sculptures out of clay, experimenting with all kinds of medium that were new to me, expanding my artistic horizons. I took the train downtown to the Art Institute of Chicago, to attend lecture classes that proved to be very beneficial. Art and music were in my comfort zone. Athletics, well that was another story. With the urging of my gym teacher, I reluctantly joined the Girls Athletic Association. We were trained to umpire baseball games during gym periods and I can still see the angry face of a senior girl as she screamed profanities at me for calling her "out." I don't think she saw me trembling, but it took a while after the game ended for me to gain my composure. Painful? Yes! But God used it to help me get over my shyness and gain self-confidence.

A highlight of my week was a Hi-Crusader Bible Club meeting on Tuesday night. Christian kids from the area gathered in a home to sing, to hear talks relating God's Word to our everyday lives and to just hang out, while snarfing down snacks and vying for the attention of the opposite sex. Roller skating parties, trips to the beach and hayrides provided fun times and great memories. One such memory was when I was snuggled in the hay next to a boy I liked, listening to the "clip-clop" of the horses hooves as the hay wagon moved along a country road. Wanting to hold hands with him, I said, "My hands are cold." "Here. You can have my gloves." That was not the response my tender teenage heart longed for.

My sister Joy and I didn't do a lot together because she was four years older than I but I loved it when she would go roller skating at an indoor roller rink and take me with her. She had a beautiful singing voice and we loved music so we were able to both be a part of a choir. Teens from all over the Chicago area met downtown every Saturday morning to sing with the

Hi-C Choral. We practiced for three hours every week, gave concerts at local churches and worked hard to prepare for our annual concert held at Orchestra Hall. Girls wore white formal dresses and guys wore tuxedos. Singing the Messiah with the Chicago Symphony Orchestra one year, was a once-in-a-lifetime opportunity.

During the summer between my junior and senior years, I decided to go to Camp Awana. I heard that the special feature during the week was to be a chalk artist named Bill Gothard. I had seen black light artists and couldn't wait to go. We played volley ball, went swimming and boating, enjoyed rowdy meals in the mess hall and were challenged by teaching sessions each morning. The evening sessions with Bill changed my life. I watched as chalk in hand, he turned the blank canvas into a work of art. As the lights dimmed, I caught my breath as a black light revealed a beautiful hidden picture illustrating a spiritual truth. I was hooked! That was what I wanted to do! Bill and I had long conversations, but not just about art. You see, for the first three years of high school, I had been a fairly "quiet Christian." After all, most of the kids in my school were Jewish and I didn't think they wanted to hear about Jesus. Bill said, "Micki, read this verse to me." He held his Bible out to me and I read, "For God has not given us the spirit of fear, but of power and of love and of a sound mind. So don't be ashamed of the testimony of our Lord." (I Timothy 1:7, KJV). Tears filled my eyes as I prayed, "Okay, Lord, You're in charge. I won't be afraid to talk about You this year." That September, red leather Bible on top of my books, I started my senior year, expecting to be ridiculed but instead my friends were curious. One day in art class Bonnie asked, "Is the story of David and Goliath really in the Bible?" I wasn't sure exactly where, but after a frantic prayer, I found it and handed her my Bible. After reading it she said, "That's amazing!" Another friend asked me to get her a New Testament. "I'll have to keep it hidden," she said, "because my mom won't want me reading it." Every now and then, she would ask me questions about Jesus because in that version of the New Testament all prophecies in the Old Testament that Jesus fulfilled were printed in red and truth penetrated her heart. Perhaps Jesus was her Messiah! Suddenly I didn't have to be silent anymore. God was using me as a vessel, pouring out His love to these His chosen people. All I had to do was allow Him to fill me and be willing to let Him use me.

During my senior year, a young man came to do radio work for the mission organization where the sponsors of my Bible club worked. I had had a special boy friend for two years but something was different about this relationship. He was four years older than I and we communicated deeply right from the start. We both longed to serve God and were trained to counsel young people who were interested in having a personal relationship with Jesus. We would talk with them following Youth for Christ rallies on Saturday nights. Hearing their prayers of repentance and seeing the joy in their faces was thrilling. Yielding to Jesus and inviting Him to live in them, made them new creations.

After my final Hi-C Choral concert in May of my senior year, he asked my parents for permission to drive me home. We drove along Lake Michigan from downtown to the North Shore where he found a beautiful spot to park. My heart pounded when he asked me to marry him and slipped a sparkling diamond ring on my finger. I said "Yes!" For me it was a dream come true, to be engaged to this very special, talented young man.

After graduation, I got a job and we both worked and prepared for a February wedding. We applied to Moody Bible Institute and were accepted for the fall term.

As a teenage bride-to-be, I had no idea what the future held, but faced it with excitement and great anticipation of what God had in store for us.

CHAPTER 3

Moody required that their students be married for six months before starting classes so we were married on a cold February Sunday afternoon, at Edgewater Baptist Church in Chicago. After a small reception at my parent's home, we spent our wedding night in our efficiency apartment and on Monday ventured out to spend our wedding gift money on exciting things like an ironing board. A honeymoon was postponed due to lack of resources but we didn't mind because we were excited to be married and on our way to Moody.

In September we were welcomed warmly by the upper classmen in the married couples dorm. Each couple had one or two rooms, shared bathrooms, and ate meals in the main dining hall. The food was served family style and we quickly discovered that if you were the last to get a serving bowl or platter, you might be out of luck! We could go to the kitchen to see if there were seconds but often were met with disappointment, not more food. First year students were required to work at the school and having experience in radio, my husband was hired to work for radio station WMBI. I was hired to work in the Service Department, filing endlessly for ninety cents an hour. The teachers were excellent and I did fine except for one class. The professor's grasp of church history was astonishing and he talked faster than I could listen. I barely passed with a D grade after he took me into his office and talked me through the written exam, a humbling experience to say the least.

Each semester we were assigned to go to some location in Chicago to serve. A favorite of mine was walking a mile to a small mission in a poor part of the city, to have a Kids Club. Graffiti, boarded up store fronts and disheveled people stumbling along pushing all their earthly belongings in old grocery carts, were images I was not used to seeing. The children would be waiting outside for us, and we would squeeze through the door with a child clinging to each arm. These little ones were thirsty for attention and needed to learn of Jesus' love. Their tragic home situations, the poverty they accepted as a normal way of life and the hunger in their hearts to know more about Jesus, touched me deeply. Mine was a middle class family and I was not accustomed to this kind of extreme need. How could I really help them? God began to open my eyes to the real world and awaken a desire to get involved.

A highlight each year was a Missions Conference, when missionaries from around the world told of their experiences and shared what God was doing to grow His kingdom worldwide.

Each year, I felt God tugging at my heart, but didn't know how to respond. In our junior year, the conference was especially powerful. In the last session, Dr. Culbertson, president of MBI, invited those who felt called to full time Christian service to stand. I felt with certainty God's hand on my shoulder. My heart pounded and tears came to my eyes. I was a married woman. How could I say "Yes" unless my husband responded to the Spirit speaking to him. Suddenly, I felt movement next to me and realized that he was standing! It was real! God was calling us to serve Him in full time ministry. I stood, slipping my hand in his and together we committed our lives to serve God. We applied to a mission agency and were accepted. Our call was to missionary radio work.

About the time the excitement of our call to missions was wearing off, God had more wonderful news for us. We were going to have a baby! Only those who have been privileged to be parents know the joy of anticipating a new life. Morning sickness made working and attending classes a bit more challenging, but the thrill of our first child made it all worthwhile.

We moved from the dorm to housing provided by our mission and in late August we welcomed our baby boy, Jerry. My babysitting jobs had been with school age children. I had never taken care of an infant, so my experience was limited to changing a diaper on a doll during a parenting class. Wow! What a shock, when I placed him on the changing table and removed his diaper. I had never even seen a baby boy. Newly circumcised, partial umbilical cord still attached, crying for all he was worth, my new little son had me in tears by the time I cleaned him up and conquered the cloth diaper, pins and rubber pants. As they say, "Practice makes perfect" and he offered many opportunities in the first few days.

Our apartment was one room, with a bed that folded down from the wall, a walk-in closet, bath, and kitchenette. The closet had a window, so that became the nursery. I took classes in the evening for my last year and we graduated the following June. The ceremony was held in Moody Church. My husband, as president of our class, addressed the graduates. I had been a Christian since childhood but at Moody I observed people who seemed to have a deeper connection with God than I. I longed for more and as I gazed at the platform, our class verse caught my eye. Large letters above the choir loft read, "That I may know Him" (Philippians 3:10, NIV). I prayed, "O God, I want to know you intimately, at any cost!" I had no idea what lay ahead of me for God to answer my prayer and learned as time passed not to pray a prayer unless I truly meant it.

We moved to Oklahoma to be close to my in-laws and for my husband to finish his degree. He started classes at the university, worked at a radio station and part time at our church. I kept busy taking care of the house and loved being a "stay-at-home" mom. As time passed, I sensed we were growing apart but thought it was just because of our different schedules. Unfortunately, it was more serious than that. One Friday evening he was lying on the couch and after putting Jerry to bed, I sat in a chair across from him, my feet curled up under me to avoid the cockroaches that scurried across the floor occasionally, freaking me out. I pressed him to tell me what was going on and was stunned by his response. The words were ones no woman ever wants to hear. Love had died and he was leaving me.

At that moment in time, the vessel of my life was shattered. I couldn't stop crying and in a few days he moved out. I found myself alone and not wanting to live. On the way to a grocery store, I stood at the curb, the cars whizzing by me. I thought, "If I just step out, my pain will be over!" But the thought of leaving Jerry was unbearable. I had not yet learned to drive, had no car, no T.V., no close friends or family. His parents didn't know what was going on so, I couldn't talk to them. It was me, my baby, and God. I went from grief to despair to anger. I said to God, "You can't do this to me! I tried to follow You faithfully and now my life is shattered. It's just not fair!" Then the Spirit led me to read Isaiah 45:9, (NIV).

"Woe to him who quarrels with his Maker, to him who is but a potsherd.....

Does the clay say to the potter, What are you making?"

The truth was that as Jeremiah had witnessed,

> "... the pot he was shaping from the clay was marred in his hands; so the potter formed it into another pot, shaping it as seemed best to him." (Jeremiah 18:4, NIV).

I was marred, even in His hands, and now he was shaping my life as seemed best to him, even though the working of the clay caused me great pain. Had I not prayed to know Him intimately, no matter what the cost?

One night, after putting Jerry in his crib, I fell to my knees by my bed. I could not go on!

At the end of myself, I cried out to God, "Lord, if I am going to go on living, you're going to have to do something!" And He did! It was as if His strong arms encircled me. Peace flooded my inner being and I rested in His indescribable love. I was his precious child, He was my heavenly Father and that would never change. With that realization, the first shattered piece of my vessel was restored- my self esteem! It didn't matter who else accepted me or rejected me. I was loved with perfect love and nothing would ever change that. I crawled into bed and slept like a baby, waking the next morning with joy in anticipation of the day, rather than dread and fear. When Jerry napped, I immersed myself in reading the Bible and it came to life in a way I had never before experienced. As the bread of life, it fed me. As the water of life, it quenched my soul thirst. I discovered passages like Job 23:10 (NIV).

"But he knows the way that I take, when he has tested me, I will come forth as gold."

I had a choice. I could either allow him to create from this chaos gold, or I could become garbage, useless to Him and others. I quickly realized that I can live without a husband, family, and friends, but I cannot live without God. He in indispensable!

I grabbed on to promises like Deuteronomy 31:8,(NIV).

"The Lord himself goes before you and will be with you; he will never leave you nor forsake you. Do not be afraid; do not be discouraged."

As the weeks passed, my hope that we would be reconciled began to waver. It would be years before reconciliation would take place between us.

I was reading a little devotional book called *Streams in the Desert*. One day, when I was feeling particularly impatient with the situation, I opened the book and for that day there was a poem:

> Sit still, my daughter, just sit calmly still.
> Nor bid these days, these waiting days as ill.
> The One who loves thee best, who plans thy way
> Has not forgotten thy great need today,
> And if He bids thee wait, 'tis sure He waits
> To prove to thee, His tender child
> His heart's great love.

How could I not trust Him, when He was so in tune to my heart needs?

As time passed, I needed income and people around me for support. I felt that perhaps it was true that "absence makes the heart grow fonder," so I moved back to my parent's home in Chicago. They were gracious and supportive and my dad especially bonded with Jerry so they became buddies. At times I sensed they were ashamed of my failed marriage and that really hurt but it was understandable.

By summer, the divorce was finalized and another wave of grief swept over me. I met with our mission agency to resign and was reminded that you don't have to cross an ocean to be useful to God.

I got a job at Baptist General Conference Headquarters in Chicago, applied to Trinity College and began to prepare for a teaching career so that I could have a schedule that would allow me to be with Jerry more than other nine-to-five jobs.

Dad helped me learn to drive but I had no car! Pastor Yaxley knew a car dealer in Rockford, about two hours drive from my house and he found a black Volkswagen that I could afford and drove it to my house, his wife following him in their car. After looking it over, I gave him a check, he gave me a receipt and $1200 worth of S&H green stamps. You may ask, "What are those?" They were stamps that you could redeem for various items like toys, household items, etc. and since I didn't have my license yet, I was more excited about the stamps than the car! I went out and sat in the car and thanked God for the gracious way that the dealer had brought it to my house and the obvious fact that this was my heavenly Father's provision for me.

Now I could start classes at Trinity College, and move forward with my life.

CHAPTER 4

As I waited for my appointment with the registrar at Trinity College, thoughts swirled through my mind. Was I crazy? How would I ever pull this off....take a full load of classes, work twenty hours a week, be both dad and mom to my precious son, work through my grief and stay spiritually healthy? I jumped up when my name was called for my interview. I don't remember much about it but two facts were crystal clear. Trinity would give me only one year of credit for my classes at Moody so I had three years of schooling ahead of me in order to get a teaching degree and as I stood to leave, the registrar said, "Since you are divorced, you may not develop any romantic relationships with our students while you are here." "I have no time or interest in dating, so you needn't worry about that," I assured her. The stigma of divorce was painful but a very real part of my life.

Mom worked two days a week, so I had to find child care for Jerry for those days. The wife of another student was interested. She had two boys, so Jerry would have playmates. The other days he stayed with Gramma. I was able to switch to twenty, rather than forty hours of work per week, so everything worked out and I began classes in September.

Getting a two year old up, dressed, fed, and in the car so that I could drop him off at the sitter's house and be in class by 8:00a.m. was challenging but most mornings we were able to kiss each other goodbye happily. Such was not always the case when I picked him up. Ann strongly believed that children must be forced to taste everything offered them, so I had to deal with much fuss on days when Jerry had to eat something he didn't like. It took years for him to get over some of those incidents but on the whole, Ann was an excellent caregiver.

Memories of those years are somewhat a blur. I have general impressions, such as how cold I got driving a Volkswagen in Chicago winters with nothing but the heat from the rear engine to warm the car. I had to bundle Jerry up and by the time I got home, my feet and hands were numb. Experiences like that help me not to take things like heaters in cars for granted.

I still have vivid memories of the day I took Jerry to Children's Memorial Hospital for a tonsillectomy. He was two years old and liked cowboys and dolls. I kissed him as he lay on the gurney and introduced him to Tommy, a little cowboy doll with a gun, holster, boots and a cowboy hat. The nurse said, "Tommy is having his tonsils out too," so he clutched him tightly and I turned away so he would not see the tears spilling down my cheeks. The doors to the surgical suite closed. My little guy was gone. Deep loneliness swept over me. Often, both parents are there when a child has surgery and although removing tonsils isn't a big deal, I still longed for a strong arm around me and someone to talk with during the procedure. It helped to pray and I was comforted knowing that my "shepherd" was there taking care of me and my little one. Jerry did just fine and especially enjoyed all the ice cream, popsicles and jello he was able to have during his recovery.

Our first summer vacation together at Bethany Beach in Michigan was great fun. It was my first time to drive out of state and with no GPS, I turned the wrong way. I ended up in Indiana not Michigan, so by the time I turned around and headed in the right direction, when we arrived at our cottage it was dark. We got ready for bed and after saying prayers and tucking Jerry in I lay down, exhausted. Before I could get used to the strange bed in an unfamiliar place, I heard a little voice. "Mommy, there are butterflies buzzing in my ears." Off with the covers, on with the light, I set to work smacking as many mosquitoes as I could find in the cottage. Insect repellent applied, a second round of hugs and kisses, lights out and finally....sleep.

Building sand castles, jumping in the waves, splashing each other and lots of laughter made trips to the beach our favorite pastime. Meals with other families that we knew and exploits only a two year old can think up, blended into a pleasurable week for both of us.

Life included frequent clashes of pleasure and pain. Often at night, Jerry would say, "Mommy, can I have my Daddy?" How do you explain divorce to a two year old? I would leave his room, my heart breaking because I could not fill the longing of his heart. My busy schedule kept me from dwelling on my situation and emotional healing was painfully slow.

Knowing the love of a husband, the intimacy of marriage, the pleasure of fingers intertwined, being held and sharing one's deepest feelings, then suddenly to have them all stripped away, is understood only by those who have experienced it. We are complex creatures and I found that keeping my emotions and spirit aligned was challenging, though I was always aware of God's presence.

A tangible evidence of His love was the gift of a very special friend. As I hurried into the little snack area provided for off campus students at Trinity, there she was. "Hi, I'm Joanne. Would you like to join me?" I was drawn to her immediately. "Yes, thank you. My name is Micki."

I sat down at her table and as we ate together, heard her story. Her mom had died of cancer when she was just sixteen years old, so she was helping her dad raise her two younger sisters. Her laugh was contagious and we soon became close friends. She got a job at BGC where I worked, so we drove together and often talked about her growing relationship with Bob.

The years passed quickly and in our senior year, as elementary education majors, we began student teaching. One day, she extended her left hand toward me so I could see the sparkling diamond announcing their engagement. Such excitement! They were to be married shortly after graduation in June.

The graduation banquet was to be held at a country club but I hated the idea of going alone. One day I commented to Irene, the receptionist at work, "I wish there was someone who would be my escort, no strings attached." She said, "I know someone who would do that for you" and in a few days, the phone rang and it was Dave, Irene's friend. Conversation flowed easily and a half hour passed unnoticed. We agreed to meet at Irene's apartment and go for pizza in Chicago's Old Town, with her and her boyfriend George. I went to her place, nervous but excited and when the two men arrived she welcomed them. One was dressed in work clothes, the other in a suit. I thought to myself, "I hope Dave is the one in the suit." He was and his warmth immediately put me at ease. Pleasant conversation sprinkled with laughter filled the evening. I relaxed with pleasure in the company of adults my age and before we parted we made plans to see each other again before the banquet.

Dave took me to the Tropical Hut near the University of Chicago. We strolled along, invigorated by the crisp night air. I slipped my arm through his, as we chatted and took in the sights.

As we drove home along Lakeshore Drive, he reached over and gently took my hand in his. I caught my breath. The pain of years with no affection from a man was eased by his gentle touch. When we arrived at my parents' home and parked out front, he reached over and turned my face toward his. As he leaned toward me I whispered, "It's been so long......" as tenderly his lips touched mine. That moment is forever etched in my mind.

The graduation banquet was a beautiful event at a local country club. The program was interesting and the food delicious. Dave was able to get to know Joanne and Bob. When she and I had a moment alone she said, "Micki, you're laughing! In all the years I've known you, you seldom laughed." I didn't realize it, but it was true. I was having fun with Dave.

When the evening ended, we stood at my front door. I thanked him for taking me and thought that our relationship might end. "I don't see why we can't continue to see each other," he said and so we did.

The next big event was my graduation from Trinity and having Dave there meant a lot.

We also celebrated when I signed a teaching contract with District 15 in Rolling Meadows, a suburb northwest of Chicago.

I needed a place to live close to my job so one Saturday I met with a realtor about places to rent and was stunned when he said, "People interested in horse racing at Arlington Race Track, rent apartments for six months, so nothing will be available until the racing season is over." I thanked him for the information and left his office not knowing what to do. A high school friend lived in Rolling Meadows. I decided to stop by Carol's house and see if she was home. After sharing my dilemma, she said, "There's a house for sale just four doors down from here. Why don't you look at it?" "How can I possibly buy a house?" I asked. "Well, it won't hurt to look at it." So as ludicrous as it seemed, the realtor came and I viewed the "matchbox house": living room – kitchen – bath – two bedrooms, perfect for Jerry and me. The former owners had not taken good care of it so the agent said, "This same house in good condition would sell for more but we're asking $13,900 for this one. The down payment is $500 but since it needs work inside and out, I'll lower it to $250. If you're interested, I need some earnest money." I couldn't believe what I was doing but it seemed that God was saying, "Here. This is my provision for you." The property opened up on a park with a creek running through it. On the other side of the creek was a pond and path leading to a school and shopping center. Two doors down was a play ground and my friend's mom who did childcare, lived around the corner. Jerry could stay with her when I had after school meetings. "How much earnest money do I need?" "Twenty dollars will do," he replied. I didn't have it so I drove to my sister's house nearby and she graciously gave me a loan. Back at the realtor's office, he explained that since I was a single mom I would need my parents to cosign the mortgage. "I can't do that. What other options do I have?" "Well, you can buy mortgage redemption insurance." So I headed home, hardly able to believe what I had just done. I was going to buy a house.

Dave and I had a date that night and I can still visualize where we were driving along in downtown Chicago when I shared my good news. "I'm buying a house!" "What? How can you even consider taking on that kind of debt?" he said. "Well there are no apartments available and the payments are less than rent would be." I don't remember what else was said but the thought went through my mind, "If he doesn't understand that this is a gift from God, then maybe he's not the one for me."

People were wonderfully supportive. The neighbors cleaned up the yard, cut the grass and trimmed the bushes. My dad painted the exterior while my mom and I painted the inside. We were able to move in, so that I could start teaching at a school just a mile away and Jerry could start first grade that September. I could trace God's hand as He perfectly fit another piece of my broken vessel in place. I had a meaningful career and a place to call home.

CHAPTER 5

The months passed quickly. Dave came to understand God was in the purchase of the house and we talked often of the future. I shared my call to full time missions work and although he had no such call, he was open to whatever God had in mind for our future. On Thanksgiving he expressed his love and asked me to marry him. I had grown to love him deeply and hoped we could share life together but knew that it depended on how he bonded with Jerry. Unless they loved and accepted each other, marriage wouldn't be wise. Jerry was already calling him "Daddy" and on Christmas Eve he proudly announced to the family that we were going to be married. What joy! God was preparing to put another piece of my vessel in place.

A popular song expresses it well.

> "And I love you so, people ask me how, how I lived 'til now – I tell them I don't know. I guess they understand how lonely life has been but life began again the day you took my hand."

On a very warm June evening, friends and family gathered at Elk Grove Baptist Church for our wedding. I walked down the aisle to the strains of Handel's Largo. We shared the traditional vows and heard those beautiful words, "I pronounce you man and wife. You may kiss your bride." Jerry sat in the front pew, his little legs swinging back and forth, as he waited to join us on the platform for a picture of our new family. A reception followed downstairs in the fellowship hall. We greeted everyone, enjoyed light refreshments and of course wedding cake. Jerry went home with my parents and we left for our honeymoon. Memories still linger of those special days of intimacy and growing in love and understanding of each other. We returned midweek and Jerry joined us for family fun at Wisconsin Dells.

Life was good. We settled into a routine, Dave adopted Jerry and in time God granted me another of my heart's desires. He blessed us with a baby girl, Cheryl Lynn. Now all of the pieces of my broken vessel were restored…. except for one.

Having a toddler and a teen, was interesting. He was a good "big brother" and Jerry was her hero. Camping with a small travel trailer and tent worked well, so together we explored many areas of our beautiful country. A visit to the Air Force Academy in Colorado, confirmed the longing in Jerry's heart to fly, so his teen years were spent preparing for a military career. Excitement filled our home the day the telegram arrived informing him of his appointment to the Air Force Academy. For me it was bitter-sweet, knowing he would soon leave our home for a very exciting future.

Adjusting to his absence was hard and I didn't realize until many years later how painful it was for Cheryl. They weren't close in age, but he was a significant part of her life and his absence left a void.

While at the Academy, Jerry met his life's partner and a few days after his graduation he and Becky were married in a beautiful ceremony in Colorado Springs. We were thrilled to have a new "daughter-in-love" and Becky became an important part of our family.

Dave worked and got his Master's degree and CPA certification attending night classes. Cheryl excelled in school and immersed herself more and more in music and drama. She was able to use her gifts one summer traveling throughout Europe with Royal Servants, an organization that took teams of teens to do evangelism. That opportunity was life changing for her. I taught preschool, led various groups at church and developed a black light chalk ministry. Using a large easel, I would draw a picture in front of a group, while music played in the background. Ahead of time, I would use invisible chalk that shows up only under a black light to draw a picture in a white area of the canvas. After sharing a Bible story, I would turn off all the lights except for the black light and a hidden picture appeared. I had seen this at camp in my teen years and now God allowed me to share His truth in a way that captivated audiences, and gave me a real high.

Before long, Cheryl graduated from high school and was accepted at Wheaton College. We entered a new phase of life – the empty nest, a very hard adjustment for this mom. It helped when our next door neighbors hired me to care for their twins, Kent and Katie. What a delight to watch them grow, become their own little people and let me pour my "motherly love" into their lives. One day at naptime as I lay on the floor between their cribs singing to them, I heard a little voice. "Micki, you stopped singing." Katie was still awake, but I had sung myself to sleep.

Another great source of joy was the arrival of Jeremy our first grandson. What fun to see our son becoming a parent. Nate arrived a few years later and although our time with them was limited because of their military lifestyle, they enlarged our lives with happy times and wonderful memories.

The empty nest offered new freedoms and Dave and I often talked of doing short-term missions trips when we retired. Then the unexpected happened.

I was no longer needed to care for Kent and Katie and found a job working with special needs children and adults at the Cabin Nature Program Center in Wood Dale. I loved nature so teaching about wild flowers, trees, mammals and reptiles was a pleasure. Programs on Indian Lore, Pioneer Life and Outdoor Cooking were challenging but fun. When I arrived home one evening, I was surprised to see Dave's car in the garage. I always got home first and as I stepped out of my car, he stuck his head out of the door which led into the kitchen and said, "You had better come inside." In the few seconds between my car and the house, all sorts of calamities flashed through my mind. Someone was hurt, terminally ill or worse...dead. I stepped into the house and into his arms. Pressing my head into his shoulder he said, "I was fired today." Relief swept over me. Our family was alright but for him, this was devastating.

We clung to each other, trying to process what this meant. How could it be? He had been with the company ten years, was the treasurer, had been given a raise not long before, and now he was terminated? It made no sense. The only explanation was that the president of the company had died and when his son took over, he wanted to bring in younger men that would take the company in a new direction. Memories of that evening are a blur. We couldn't help but ask, "Where are you, God?" The next Monday, Dave's search for a job began and we moved through the next few months, taking one day at a time. I increased my hours and during my lunch breaks walked in the woods, crying out to God but heard nothing but silence. Dave was 53 years old, not a good age to be seeking a new job. Companies were very impressed with his experience and qualifications, but were looking for someone younger.

I stood by, helpless. For the first time in our marriage Dave became depressed. He had faithfully provided for our family and had a financial plan in place for the future but now all that changed. We sought help and were frustrated when the counselor said, "Be honored that God is trusting you with His silence." We didn't want silence. We wanted answers! After a few months working for a man who had questionable ethics, Dave was invited to work part time in the missions department of Baptist General Conference. Every day he had conversations with missionaries and when he came home would say, "They are really great people." After a few months, the Midwest Office of the Conference needed an accountant so he made that change and now was interacting with pastors of churches in the Midwest.

One night he said to me, "Do you think we should investigate mission organizations and not wait until we retire?" "Yes," I said my heart pounding. This was why God had been silent. He had been patiently changing Dave's heart by having him talk to missionaries and then to pastors with whom we needed to connect in order to present our ministry to gain prayer and financial support.

We met with two mission organizations and both were interested in us. After dozens of doors at secular companies slammed shut, the door to missionary service swung wide open. We cautiously began to share what was happening and were met with interesting responses. "You can't go! I won't let you." "Go for it!" "Are you sure you are missionary material?" Obviously the road ahead would not be easy but we knew unmistakably that God was in this.

The applications for Greater Europe Mission arrived first so rather than try to apply to two organizations at the same time, we focused on GEM. The process was intense including psychological tests, thorough background information and a challenging exercise asking us to explain our doctrinal beliefs about numerous topics and back them up with scripture. During those months, our excitement grew and we began to understand the gravity of the step we were taking. On a Friday evening, we were to share our story at the end of a week of Candidate Orientation. It happened to be our wedding anniversary so we decided to interact rather than share individually. When everyone had finished they announced that we were going to be advised as to our standing with the mission, so one at a time, individuals or couples were called to the back of the room to meet with mission representatives. Suddenly, I lost it and went out into the hall. "What if they say they are rejecting us as missionaries? How humiliating would that be? But, if they say we are accepted, we are going to have to leave family, friends and our home for years to go to a place we've never been."

Finally, I could procrastinate no longer. Dave took my hand and when they called our names we walked toward the mission representative. He smiled, extended his hand and said, "Welcome to GEM." Excitement and joy flooded me. We were now official missionary candidates. That night God lovingly fit the last piece in place. I was whole, the newly formed vessel that He desired. In His time, His loving hands had shaped me exactly according to His perfect plan.

CHAPTER 6

As new appointees we were asked to represent GEM at a Missions Conference at a church in Milwaukee, Wisconsin. We were hosted by a church family and Dave commuted back to work two days while I stayed for different sessions including a women's brunch where I made a black-light presentation. We also set up a display explaining GEM's ministries throughout Europe. After the Sunday morning service a representative from their missions team came to us and thanked us for our participation. She invited us to select a cheese ball or log from a basket as a token of their appreciation. Usually in this type of situation the conference participants are given an envelope containing a check, which we were expecting since we had been there for several days. As we drove home I said to Dave, "Do you think the cheese ball is all we are getting?" "They will probably mail a check," he said.

In the days that followed we enjoyed cheese and crackers while waiting in vain for a check. You see, our heavenly Father wisely gave us cheese, the first time we went to a church to raise support, humbling us so that our expectations from that point forward were to expect little, but give much in our service because, after all, He is the one who provides in His own time and way.

We felt it would be a good idea to have a group to regularly pray with us, hold us accountable in our support raising and keep us on track. Once a month we met in our home and one urgent prayer request was for someone to rent our home for the years we would be in Europe. After several months, one of the couples lingered after the others left. As we talked together Kathy said, "We feel God is leading us to move into your home. It's a mile from church, a block from our children's school and the basement is perfect for me to set up an office to do medical billing." We were overjoyed! We trusted them and would not have to search any further for renters. Again we were affirmed that our call to missions was certain.

Support raising was a constant challenge. As we mailed out letters to friends and family, there were certain ones we felt confident would commit to pray and give. However, as time passed many of the ones we were counting on never responded, proving once again that "God's ways are not our ways." He often whispered in our spirits, "Trust me."

Our son, being in the Air Force, attended Officer's Christian Fellowship meetings. From time to time he would ask for prayer for our support needs and preparations to leave for Germany. A young officer in the group knew that the Air Force Chapel didn't need his tithe and felt God would have him join our support team. Another young woman officer felt the same and soon both were sending us generous monthly support which continued throughout our missionary career. We came to know them through letters and emails they sent regularly. We have never met face to face but grew to love them and look forward to meeting them in heaven. We watched our support grow, coming from a myriad of sources including five churches, individuals and money from the rental of our home. Equally important was our prayer support team, those people committing to pray, knowing that only with God's power working in and through us would kingdom work be accomplished.

"Stuff" was another big challenge. For Dave it was clothes, books and his computer. No problem. The other 90% of what filled our home was mine….art supplies, crafts, collections of all sorts, memorabilia from 33 yrs of marriage and child rearing. We were told to take enough things to feel at home but to keep in mind that you pay to ship everything. Furniture was expensive in Europe so we took basic furniture and 120 boxes of necessities in a small container. We found some people willing to store some things, sold others and donated much so the house was finally empty. I cried as I watched a truck full of "my stuff" drive away. Interestingly, my devotional reading for that day included the story of the man who sold everything he owned to purchase a pearl of great price. At that moment I opened my hands, let go of my stuff and received the pearl of ministry that God was giving me. As I did, a sense of freedom swept over me. I realized that God's ways are good.

As our time of departure grew closer, goodbyes became harder. Dave's family gathered for a Bon-Voyage party. Nancy, my sister-in-love had everyone who was there write a brief message, took their picture and created a memory book for us to take with us. The idea of years apart was hard for all of us to grasp.

Our next door neighbors invited us for a cook-out and when we arrived we were greeted by "Surprise!" Thirty of our neighbors had gathered to wish us well and the children in the neighborhood who for many years had come to our home for a Happy Birthday Jesus Party at Christmas, made a long banner which read "God Bless You on Your Mission." Not all of them understood the concept of our becoming missionaries but they knew that we loved God and were leaving to go serve Him in Germany.

My Dad, a widower in his 90's, struggled the most with our leaving and our last few visits were bitter-sweet. As we sat together I recorded his voice as he shared memories of his childhood, teen years and other things that were important to him. I also played some of his favorite hymns on the piano and tears filled my eyes, as he sang along in his aging voice. I knew I was being obedient to my heavenly Father, but it was still painful to leave my earthly father.

A last visit with Jerry and Becky and our grandsons Jeremy and Nate was memorable and the parting eased by their promise to come and visit us in Germany. We knew that their marriage was strong, his military career was going well and God was blessing them in their life together.

Our daughter was single and living in Chicago so I went to the local train station to go downtown for a last visit with her. As I waited for the train, I began to chat with a group of women from Canada. As I explained where I was going tears came and before I knew it, they were tearfully hugging me and sympathizing with me over having to leave my precious daughter. I still have a Canadian coin they gave me by which to remember them. Cheryl and I did some shopping, Dave joined us for dinner but as the evening passed, the inevitable time came, when we had to say good-bye. We clung to each other and I tried to pray and share the verses, "The Lord bless you and keep you..." but sobs choked my words and after a final kiss I got in the car and we drove away. I cried all the way home. The thought of being apart for two years broke my heart. That moment revealed to me the painful cost of obedience to God's call. Later the Spirit brought to mind that Jesus experienced much greater pain when He was on the cross and the Father turned His face away from His only begotten Son because my sin was laid upon Him. As our departure grew closer, I lived in the beautiful reality that God understood perfectly all I was experiencing – the painful good-byes – the stress of leaving for the unknown – the excitement of new experiences and the joy of obedience. Not many people in midlife have such an opportunity and I was profoundly grateful.

CHAPTER

7

As the 747 aircraft heading for Frankfurt, Germany left the ground, I realized my call to missions was finally a reality. What joy! Still my heart ached as I faced the fact that my dad, almost ninety years old, my son and his family and my single daughter would soon be an ocean away. Mission policy was "no visitors and no trips home during the first two years" and that seemed like an eternity to me. Some had asked me, "How can you leave your family at this stage of life?" Humanly, I had no good answer until God in His mercy showed this verse.

> "Anyone who loves their father or mother more than me is not worthy of me; anyone who loves their son or daughter more than me is not worthy of me…" (Matthew 10:37, NIV).

The choice was clear. I had learned earlier that the "pot" has no right to question the potter. Yielding to the work of his hands brings beauty, completeness, and a sweet sense of peace.

The flight to Europe from Chicago was in the evening, so after enjoying dinner, the lights were dimmed and with blanket, pillow, earplugs and mask in place I attempted to sleep. Not Dave, though! He had to stay awake to help the pilot, in case he was needed and gripped the armrests firmly, each time there was a bump. Because of the time change, lights came on in what was the middle of our normal night and the announcement, "It's morning! Time for breakfast," brought me to consciousness.

Our excitement grew when we heard, "Ten minutes to landing." God had opened a new door for us and we were about to walk off the plane into adventures never dreamed of before. Safely through customs, we claimed our luggage, found our way out of the terminal and hailed a taxi to take us to the hotel where the annual conference for Greater Europe Mission was being held. As the driver sped along the expressway at speeds I had never experienced, I thought to myself, "Has God brought me safely all this way only for me to die in the first five minutes in Germany?" Obviously that was not the case, but it took awhile after exiting the cab for my heart to stop racing.

Inside the hotel, we were warmly welcomed by GEM staff. I could hardly believe that I was a "missionary"! The church tends to elevate those who serve God away from home but, in reality we are very ordinary people just working in other places where God plants us.

The main sessions were held in the hotel ballroom. Hundreds had gathered from all over Europe, to worship, hear what God was doing, and be fed from God's Word. Words fail when I try to describe the singing…rich male voices blended with women's voices in harmony, praising the Lord they each were committed to serve without reservation.

Halfway through the conference we met with our field director and were told our first assignment was to go south to Kandern, Germany and find housing. When the week ended, we knew that Operation Mobilization loaned cars to missionaries and we needed one to use until we could buy one. We took a train to their office in Brussels, Belgium. After staying one night, we set out in a vehicle they provided for us. Not far from the garage, the engine kept dying so we returned for another car. Other than slipping gears occasionally, it was fine and we drove to Kandern on the Autobahn – a hair-raising experience.

After settling in at a guesthouse, we bought a newspaper and opened it to what appeared to be the "want ads." One slight problem was…neither of us knew any German! Thank God for dictionaries. Paper and book in hand, the next morning we ventured to a larger city on the Swiss border, about twenty minutes from Kandern. We found a cafeteria, purchased tea and coffee and spread the paper out to begin the search for our new home, painstakingly translating each word. A realtor showed us a few apartments in that area but none were quite right. Since I had my chalkboard, I needed a place where I could practice and let the chalk dust fly. Nothing we were shown provided such a space.

On Sunday we attended the international church that Black Forest Academy provided for their English speaking staff and students. When the service ended, a GEM missionary approached us and asked, "Is anyone helping you find housing?" From the look on our faces she knew the answer was "No." She immediately arranged to meet us the next morning to help with our search. We knew God had a home for us but having a German speaker come alongside was a great encouragement. The next day she took us to see more places, but none were quite right. We had heard from a fellow missionary that there was an apartment available in the building where his family lived so midweek, when they returned from vacation, we drove to Feuerbach, a village over the hill from Kandern. We climbed the thirty-two steps to the front door, rang the bell, and were warmly welcomed. We followed them up thirty-two more steps into the vacant apartment. In Europe when a place is vacated the renters take the kitchen and bathroom fixtures because they have to purchase them when they move in. I stared in amazement at the complete kitchen, carpeted floors, beautiful bathroom and picturesque views from every window. To the east, one could see a forested mountain…to the west, sunset over the Rhine Valley…to the north and south, vineyards and orchards. I love nature and I began to weep as I realized that my heavenly Father had provided this setting for me. That wasn't all! Our friends showed us another flight of stairs leading up to an attic, half finished and the other half unfinished. This would be my art studio! God knew exactly what we needed and that afternoon, tenderly unwrapped his precious gift – our new home in Germany! I still get emotional each time I return to Feuerbach, my "other home." I have no patience when people talk to me about the "sacrifices" I made to leave my beautiful house here to go to Germany. I know it is not true for many missionaries, but for us this was no sacrifice. Our home in Rolling Meadows was rented by a family from our church, so we knew we would return there eventually.

Someone had left a foam couch that could be unfolded for sleeping so we decided to move in, even though the container of our belongings would not arrive for a couple of weeks. With a set of camping dishes, an iron skillet, a patio table and two folding chairs loaned by other missionaries along with a couple of towels, we were "good to go." We brought home our plastic coffee cups from the drink machine at language school. One day when I was complaining that I had no ice cubes, the little boy from downstairs said, "Why don't you use a plastic egg carton?" Perfect idea! It was great fun learning how to improvise like grilling toast when there is no toaster and cutting off the bottom of plastic bottles to make drinking glasses. Interestingly, when our container arrived with all our "stuff," I bemoaned the fact that I had brought so much having just learned how little I really need to live.

Each morning we rode the train to Freiburg, to take German classes. For us in midlife, learning a new language was quite a humbling experience. We sat at a u-shaped table with about twenty students from many different countries. I tried to hide behind Dave so that the teacher wouldn't call on me but it didn't work. He moved from one student to the next, trying hard to get all of us to participate. Making sounds my mouth had never made before didn't come easily especially when others were staring at me. Because many languages were represented, he used only German to teach and would answer our questions in English at break time.

Eventually we changed to evening classes which were less intense but in one situation provided more excitement. The class was held in a multi-story building in Lorrach, the city where we first searched for an apartment.

One evening we decided to have a bite to eat before heading home, so we each went into our respective restrooms. When we came out, everyone had left including the instructor. We attempted to open the door leading to the stairs that led to the exit but it was locked from the outside. We searched for another way out, but to no avail. There was a balcony at the front of the classroom so I stepped out and looked down to see if there was anyone on the street below.

A man was standing by his car talking on a cell phone so I called out to him, "Hilfe, Hilfe!" But he ignored my cry for help, got into his car and drove away. I began to panic. What if no one helped us? What if we had to spend the night there? Dave found another small balcony and called to a man on his garage roof next door. After great effort he was able to communicate enough so that he understood our predicament and called the police. They in turn were able to contact the hausmeister who came with a set of keys and let us out. It wasn't fun but provided a good story for us to tell our German friends and family at home.

I was adjusting to my new home, but really missed family and friends. My close friend's birthday was coming so I prepared a small package and card to send to her. Dave offered to take it to the Post Office and I told him to be sure and send it so that she would have it on her birthday. However, when he returned he said that it was "too expensive," so he sent it surface mail which would take several weeks. I am not a person who is easily angered but at that moment, I lost it! I yelled at him and ran from the house sobbing. The road out of our village was lined on one side with vineyards and on the other, fields ripe for harvest. I found a bench under a tree and plopped down trying to control my tears. As I sat there, I became aware of someone singing. Wiping my eyes to see more clearly, I saw a farmer and his wife in the gently sloping field in front of me. He was digging in the soil and she knelt, picking up potatoes and tossing them in a basket. As he worked he sang, the sound of his rich bass voice reaching my ears. The German lyrics were unknown to me but I clearly understood the words my heavenly Father spoke to my heart in that moment. I was His precious child and needed to stop my tears and start to serve Him with joy. I trudged up the gravel road to our house, climbed the sixty-four steps to our apartment and buried my tear stained face in Dave's shoulder as he held me. "I'm sorry I yelled and got angry. Please forgive me." "It's okay. I'm sorry I didn't do what you asked," and his tender kiss made things right.

My missionary journey changed that day. One after the other, God gave me beautiful opportunities for ministry that I will share in the pages that follow and in all the seven years that I lived in Feuerbach, I never again heard a farmer singing. He was there that day because God wanted to use his song to touch my heart.

CHAPTER 8

Weeks passed and we watched as God with an artist's palette painted the world around us with brilliant hues. The forests – red, orange, yellow…the fields of grain – golden…the vineyards – deep purple, burgundy and pale green.

Learning German was painfully slow prompting us to drive to Lorrach where there were large supermarkets so I could buy packaged meat and avoid going to the local butcher, where I had to ask for what I wanted. Realizing that wasn't practical, I learned how to ask for a pound of ground beef and with fear and trembling went to the butcher. "Guten Tag," I said. "Ich mochte ein halb kilo hackfleisch, bitte" which means "Good day. I would like a half kilo ground beef, please."

The woman behind the counter smiled and said, "Mochten sie Rindfleisch oder Rindfleisch und Schweinefleisch gemischt?"

I wasn't prepared for any questions and stuttered "uh I don't speak much German," to which she replied in perfect English, "Would you like beef or beef and pork mixed?" So it went, speaking sometimes correctly and other times not.

Teenagers howled with laughter at our pronunciation and the five year old downstairs made it her job to try and teach us the new words she learned in kindergarten each day, enthusiastically correcting our pronunciation.

Attending church on Sundays was the highlight of our week. The service was at Black Forest Academy a school taught in English for missionary kids or expatriates living in the area.

Shortly before Christmas, I met Katherine, a Canadian missionary, who taught piano lessons to children in the community, to build relationships with Germans. She heard about my chalk drawings and asked if I would come and draw at a recital while her students performed. Thrilled to have an open door, I said, "Of course. When I finish and turn the black light on may I share about God's gift of His Son Jesus?" "Yes," she said. "That would be perfect." The recital was a success and afterward a German woman approached me. "Hello" she said. "My name is Renate. I spent the senior year of high school in Minneapolis as a foreign exchange student. I worked at A&W Root Beer." That conversation was the beginning of a beautiful friendship. We discovered that her parents, brother and sister, all lived next door to us in Feuerbach. In time we were invited to birthday parties, were asked to videotape her brother's wedding and attended many concerts presented by the Harmonika Orchestra directed by her husband Walter. She and most of her family were all musicians and we were fascinated by the beautiful sound created by accordions as they played classical selections, American 50's tunes and traditional German folk tunes. A Budenfest was held each September in Kandern's central plaza. Booths were constructed by each musical group from the surrounding villages and delicious taste treats were for sale. We helped serve Kaffee and Kuchen at the orchestra's booth. Dave bussed tables and I poured endless cups of coffee. The bond between us and our German friends deepened as they saw our willingness to work hard alongside of them.

Walter and Renate are close friends who
we enjoyed meals with often.

Our first Christmas away from home was bitter-sweet. We enjoyed the many festive decorations, concerts and the Christmas markets. Often held in the town's main square, dozens of booths displayed an amazing assortment of things to buy. Handcrafted Christmas ornaments, hand blown glass decorations and beautifully carved wooden nutcrackers, were just a few of the gifts to be purchased. Gingerbread cookies in all shapes and sizes, chestnuts freshly roasted, candies of all sorts, bratwurst and mugs of hot mulled wine teased our taste buds. I sat down to rest and "people watch." I looked at their feet, as they hurried by me and I began to think about feet from long ago.

~the swollen feet of Mary, about to deliver her first born
~the aching feet of Joseph as he trudged from inn to inn searching for a place to rest
~the tiny wrinkled feet of the newborn king, tenderly kissed by his mother
~the callused feet of the shepherds as they ran to see what the angels had announced
~the manicured feet of the royal visitors that brought rich gifts to the young child
~the pacing feet of Herod as he screamed his hatred toward this unwelcome threat to his throne
~the bloodied feet of the soldiers who carried out his edict among the screams of mothers
~the gentle feet of Jesus as he grew and walked among those whom He had made
~the nail pierced feet of our Savior, dying to fulfill the reason He'd been born, to pay for our sin

As Paul wrote, "how beautiful are the feet of those who bring glad tidings" (Romans 10:15, NIV).

I stood up, realizing that was why I was celebrating Christmas in Germany rather than at home. The pain of separation eased and the joy of the season filled my heart.

Shortly after Christmas we heard about the need for chaperons to go to Krackow, Poland with a team of BFA students. They were preparing to present the gospel through mime and I realized that my chalk drawings would enhance their ministry. When Easter break arrived, we found ourselves bouncing along in a school van surrounded by talkative teens. Their singing and chatter helped the hours pass quickly. We stayed at an old Communist hotel and after our first breakfast consisting of half-cooked scrambled eggs and bread, we headed out to do some sightseeing. We drove to Lublin where Majdanek Concentration Camp was located. We were all curious as to what it was like. The first barrack we entered was filled with display cases of personal belongings taken from the prisoners. Combs, toothbrushes, wallets, small trucks, stuffed animals and dolls. Above the cases were photos of children whose hands had been pried open as they clutched their one last precious possession. My eyes filled with tears and I pushed my way outside, unable to bear seeing any more. How could any human being treat innocent children that way?

Afraid of what I would see next, I hesitated to enter the next barrack but knew I needed to stay with the group so I went in. There reaching from floor to ceiling were wire cages filled with shoes taken from prisoners. Some of the 800,000 shoes…all sizes…women's shoes, baby shoes, men's work boots that had been found after liberation, were on display. My mind couldn't grasp how many innocent people those shoes represented. Stepping outside my eyes were drawn to a rough statue.

A statue at Majdanek Concentration Camp
showing the love of a mother trying to
protect her child from the gas fumes

A woman, her arms stretching high above her head, held her baby as she tried to keep her from the deadly gas fumes, rising from the floor. The sick feeling in my stomach grew and spotting a student who was deeply touched by all she was seeing, I slipped my arm around her waist and tried to comfort her. As we approached the far end of the camp we spotted a huge round canopy covering a circular mound. A sign explained that this was ash from some of the hundreds of thousands of people burned in the ovens there. Everyone was moved to tears at the enormity of the atrocities we had seen. One by one we turned and made our way to the entrance, some alone, some with arms around each other but all silent. None of us had been prepared for what we had seen and to "flee" was a natural response.

That afternoon we had a debriefing session, shared our feelings, prayed for the relatives of those who had died there and for those we would be reaching with the hope of the Gospel.

Souvenir shopping lightened our spirits and supper at our first Polish shopping mall was an interesting cultural experience.

As we prepared for bed I said to Dave, "You may have to take care of me tonight. I feel awful." "I may not be of much help," he said. " I feel sick to my stomach." Without going into detail, we spent one of the worst nights of our lives suffering from food poisoning, probably from the half-cooked eggs we ate at breakfast. By morning we both almost felt death might be a welcome alternative to what we were experiencing. Our hosts shared some Polish remedies but Dave did not respond. He was destined for a day in the room. The team was to drive out into the countryside to a village school where I was to draw a chalk picture. I knew there wouldn't be "comfort stations" along the way, so the team gathered around me praying that God would stop the diarrhea and vomiting. In His mercy He touched me and enabled me to make the trip. We were welcomed by a very excited group of children who had never seen any Americans and watched as they sat mesmerized as I drew and shared the story of Jesus' love for them. God intervened so that His purpose could be fulfilled.

Back at the hotel, some of my symptoms returned and it took most of the remainder of the trip for us to gain full strength. The students had several opportunities to use mime to visualize the difference Jesus makes in our lives when we trust in Him and on the way home we celebrated the wonder of having seen God work in and through us to touch lives.

CHAPTER 9

The trip from Germany to Poland was long so the excitement of our team grew when we saw signs along the road for Camp Ostrada. As we turned in none of us were prepared for the beauty of the sun dancing on the lake, the trees, flowers and serenity of the campgrounds.

We had come to teach English to a group of teens from Belarus but more importantly to share the love of Jesus with them. This was a unique group of young people who had suffered much growing up under Communism. If that wasn't enough, they were young children when the Chernobyl disaster took place. Radioactive material was released into the atmosphere but the Russians failed to warn anyone. Winds carried it over Belarus and when it rained, a foamy substance came down and curious children played with it, tasted it and unknowingly exposed themselves to radiation. As they grew, most became very ill with thyroid cancer and those who survived were shunned because of their condition. They had to live with hair loss, scars from surgery and prolonged illness. These were to be our students and before turning in for the night we met as a team to pray.

The next day we welcomed them warmly but found them slow to make eye contact and somewhat ill at ease. They were used to living in a country decimated by violence, resulting in poverty, alcoholism and hopelessness. The contrast of this beautiful natural setting, warm welcoming people, comfortable cabins and abundant food, soon caused them to relax and open up. The English classes included a reading from the New Testament. For many it was the first time they had read God's Word. I couldn't even begin to grasp what it was like to grow up in a Godless environment or what it was like to read the gospel of John for the first time. They simply read it as a reading exercise and it became a good source of discussion at meals as they asked questions and tried to understand its meaning.

The days passed quickly. Swimming and boating were favorites and the casual atmosphere provided opportunities for our students to use the English they were learning in conversations. During group time, at first some were slow to sing but fun songs drew them in and soon they were enthusiastically singing worship songs. Each team member shared their story which was translated to make sure they understood. Sharing what life was like before we met Jesus, how we came to trust in Him as our Savior and the difference knowing Him makes in our everyday lives, made our stories personal and unique.

As the two weeks drew to a close, an evening around a campfire was a highlight. Both teachers and students shared what this camp experience meant to them. No one wanted the evening to end because we knew that the next morning we would be saying good-bye. These precious young people stepped out of their van into the sunlight of a beautiful natural setting but more importantly into the "Sonlight" of being introduced to Jesus – the light of the world.

The next day the reality of having to return to Belarus brought many of them to tears.

They clung to us and our tears flowed freely as we felt the depth of their sadness. Unable to delay any longer, they reluctantly climbed in the van and we waved good-bye until they were out of sight.

Standing there we feared we would never see them again this side of heaven. We knew some were believers but not all and this gave us the incentive to pray diligently for each one. Little did we know that a few months later we would be invited to Belarus for a reunion with our students. A church there sponsored us and so we found ourselves once again hugging and laughing as many of our students welcomed us, overjoyed at being together again. We stayed in an old communist hotel and were not allowed to leave the premises without our official guide. We shared meals and fellowship at the church, went for long walks around the city and were treated to two very special events. The Bolshoi Ballet was performing the Nutcracker so for five dollars we had a superb cultural experience. The next night the students were even more excited as they ushered us into the stadium to see the Russian Circus. Clowns, precision-trained horses ridden by exquisitely dressed acrobats and acts including many other animals amazed us. I can still see the final act in my mind's eye. A huge net surrounding the center ring slowly rose vertically from floor to ceiling. Next large balls were rolled out into the ring and with the crack of a whip white tigers raced in. Each mounted a ball and were kept busy balancing themselves as the trainer took turns doing amazing tricks with each one. For the finale a ball was lowered from the ceiling and we watched spellbound, as a tiger and his trainer mounted the ball and it ascended high into the air. The audience burst into applause when the ball descended and the trainer took a bow. Our conversation going back to the hotel was filled with appreciation for the evening and the ingenuity of the people. Our young students beamed with pride because we were so impressed. The next day we gathered at the church to sing and pray and were thrilled to hear that some of them had come to trust Christ. After more tearful good-byes we returned home. In the days that followed as I thought about my experiences with the Belarusians God renewed my awareness of His sovereignty. He has a plan for every individual and He loves them with a perfect love.

I was back in Germany but felt frustrated. Going to other places for ministry was exciting but I longed for opportunities in our community. God knows our heart's desires and soon I was invited to draw for a special event at a home for seniors in Kandern. I spent hours preparing. I practiced my chalk drawing and had the story of God's Trees translated and recorded by a German friend. The tape would play while I was drawing. The day came, warm and beautiful. The event was outdoors so I set up my easel on the patio and gave the taped story to the German man in charge of the sound system. Residents of the home, families and people from the village gathered and the program began. When introduced, I greeted them and asked them to start the tape. My heart pounded as I realized that nothing was coming out of the speakers. My friend checked the tape and restarted it, but the result was the same. Silence! I fought back tears. How could this be happening? Somehow the man had erased the tape. Another missionary's daughter came up and said, "I know that story. Shall I tell it while you draw?" "Oh yes, please," I said and started frantically drawing, trying to keep up with her version.

I kept from sobbing until I was in the car on the way home. I can't describe how humiliated I felt. I was a representative of the dozens of missionaries who lived in that community and taught at Black Forest Academy but more importantly, I was a believer and so wanted to honor the Lord Jesus.

For weeks, I didn't want to go to the store or be seen in Kandern because I didn't know who would recognize me. What happened that day did not catch God by surprise. I don't know what He did in others but He certainly showed me that His ways are very different from our ways. I wasn't aware that I was proud of my chalk ministry but if there was pride in my heart, that incident erased it, just as the story was erased from the tape.

Every year, Black Forest Academy invited the German people in the community to a Candlelight Dinner. The school was built after World War II to provide a place for the children of missionaries and expatriates living in the region to have an education in English. Through the years the community grew to appreciate the school so people were quick to come to these special events. English speakers were welcome but it was understood that we would invite German friends and neighbors to be our guests. Soon I was immersed in art projects needed for the dinner. The student body and staff of the school provided a great source of talent and each year a program was planned, often with an American 50's theme which the Germans loved. During the program there was always a clear presentation of the Gospel, real and relevant to everyday life. One year a staff member rode his Harley onto the stage and dressed in his leathers, shared how his personal relationship with Jesus made a difference in everyday life. Good food, lots of laughter and great music combined to make a most enjoyable evening.

One year we brought a young married couple who were our neighbors as our guests. During the dessert course, he turned to me and said, "Jesus, Jesus, Jesus! That's all you talk about! What about God?" That was a perfect opportunity to explain the basis of our faith. Taking a pen from my purse I drew two parallel lines on the paper tablecloth explaining that the lower line was earth and the one above it was heaven. He agreed that God is holy and we are not and then we talked about good people and I represented them with arrows reaching up toward heaven from earth. After some discussion he agreed that no one is as good as God. "That poses a problem," I said. "But God, because of His great love for us, sent His only Son, Jesus, to take the punishment for our imperfections on Himself and die on the cross." At that point I drew the cross connecting the two lines. "In John 14:6, (NIV), Jesus answered, 'I am the way and the truth and the life. No one comes to the Father except through me'. That is why we focus on Jesus." The music began for the second half of the program and so the discussion ended. Only God knows if he has placed his faith in Jesus, but hopefully it gave him food for thought. I am so thankful that all God asks of me is to sow the seed and leave the rest to Him.

CHAPTER 10

Romania! I really don't know where to begin. I went there five times for different kinds of ministry and somehow the people wrapped themselves around my heart. I had never seen such poverty, yet the people had such strength and capacity to love and to be loved, that I was drawn back there.

The roads there were the worst I had ever experienced. There were no shoulders but a middle lane that traffic in both lanes used for passing. You can imagine the fear that gripped us when the driver of our van, carrying a team of teachers, pulled into the center lane to pass and suddenly a car going the other direction, pulled out facing us head on. It tested our faith big time and kept us praying continually.

Our destination was Camp Bradatel, a beautiful spot at the edge of a National Forest. Our route took us through many villages where cows and pigs had the right-of-way. We passed some large ornate houses and were told by our host that they were owned by gypsies who traveled all around Europe often sleeping in tents or their cars. They used these homes to display their wealth often gained in questionable ways. We passed one intersection of two roads and as far as you could see there was nothing but rubble, the remains of homes that the communists had destroyed when they forced the people to leave and move into multi-story concrete tenements. Able to take only what they could carry, they lost most of their belongings including animals that were left behind. The years under Communism broke the will of many people who turned to alcohol in their distress, destroying many families. They had gained their freedom not long before we arrived and now hope of a better life filled their hearts. You could see it on their faces and hear it in their voices.

A stream flowed along the side of the road that led into the camp and we were told that we would not be able to communicate by email or phone once we reached our location unless we were driven out of the valley. This was the first time since moving to Germany that Dave and I had been away from each other so it was hard to not be able to call him. The church had purchased the property from the government and I was soon distracted with getting settled into my room in the barracks that had been built for construction workers to live in while they built a dam in the area. This was no Ritz Carlton but it was clean. We toured the camp and learned that hot showers were only available at certain times, when they would heat water from the creek for your allotted 5 minutes.

The laundry for the camp was done in a huge barrel-like container through which creek water flowed - a unique system I can't really describe but it did the job. Meals were served in a mess hall, family style, and various rooms provided teaching space. After dinner we met and prayed for our students, anticipating what God would do in the next two weeks.

The vans pulled in early the next day and soon there was a group of teens, chattering in Romanian. They explored their new surroundings, excited about being away from home and ready for the challenge of learning English. We grouped them according to their ability, introduced them to their teachers and sent them off for their first classroom experience. After lunch, basketball, soccer & volleyball gave them a chance to let off steam and then more classes filled the time until dinner. In the evening we had group time with skits, songs and team members telling how Christ had become a vital part of his or her life. I brought my black-light easel and one night drew a picture for them. I shared how God allowed me to be broken and step by step put the vessel of my life back together.

The students gazed intently at the picture that showed up when I turned on the black light and they saw Jesus' fingers on the rim of a vessel, once lying in pieces now made whole by His touch. I closed in prayer and they quietly left the room. I felt the presence of the Holy Spirit and prayed that God would work in their hearts. The next day after lunch my team leader came and said, "There is a student who would like to talk with you. Would this be a good time?" "Sure," I said as she led me toward a young man. She introduced him and Alin and I strolled down to the gazebo by the river. We chatted, his limited knowledge of English a challenge but not enough to keep him from sharing the news.

"Last night I trusted Jesus as my Savior." Chills ran up and down my spine as I realized God had worked and now this young man would spend eternity in heaven. I could see the joy in his eyes and we prayed together and met several times during the week to talk about what it meant to be a follower of Christ. We never know what God will use...a word...a song...a picture... a verse of scripture, to reveal His truth to a lost person and shine the light of salvation into their spirit.

A year later, I was at camp again and was thrilled when, on the weekend I was told I had a visitor and there, walking toward me, was Alin. He had come to visit and I was able to meet his mother, sisters and brother-in-law and was pleased that he brought his guitar and played for me. It is hard to describe the heart connection between us but it is sweet. We exchange emails and I am happy to say that through the years we have stayed in touch even exchanging birthday and Christmas greetings. Through photos I have seen him mature, graduate from college, get married, have a son and serve the Lord faithfully through his church. We pray for each other and he is a source of great joy in my life. We may not meet face-to-face again on this earth, but I look forward with great anticipation, to someday seeing my "son-in-the-Lord" in heaven.

The following year, Alin made a surprise visit to camp, brought his guitar and played for me.

CHAPTER 11

"We're taking a medical team to Romania this fall. How about going with us?" Our fellow missionaries explained that church planters, working in small villages with shepherd families, needed a team of nurses and other qualified people to come and help meet the physical needs of the villagers with whom they were trying to share the gospel. Jesus often healed bodies as well as souls and this sounded intriguing to us. "We have no medical training so how can we help?" "You can provide practical assistance and spiritual encouragement to the team and share the love of Jesus with the Romanians," they said. As we prayed about it and talked with friends from our church, two nurses came and said, "We want to go with you." This was just what we needed to see that God wanted us out of our comfort zone and experiencing something new.

Kathy and Sue had no trouble getting the financial and prayer support that they needed and before long we had a full team of paramedics and nurses who collected medical supplies to take to help those in need. An organization called "Shoes for Orphan Souls," shipped boxes of shoes for us to distribute, as well as one hundred stuffed lambs with the message "Jesus loves you" to give to children. Our church commissioned us for our ministry and we left, excited but not knowing exactly what to expect.

On a previous trip to Romania, I arrived but my suitcase didn't. I had three interesting days dressed like a villager in worn, out of style clothes sent from churches in America. Thankfully, both Sue and Kathy had a great sense of humor because Sue's suitcase didn't show up for several days. They had fun figuring out what they could find for Sue to wear which was the right size, from among the clothes the team had brought with them.

The first night, after getting settled in our rooms, we gathered for fellowship and prayer, and to hear the church planter's vision of what our team would accomplish. I was moved by their enthusiasm and anticipation of what God would do. They worked alone so having a group of believers surrounding them energized and lifted their spirits.

The next morning we traveled to a nearby village where the doctor opened the doors of his clinic and welcomed us warmly. Villagers who had heard we were coming were already waiting for an opportunity to have some much needed free medical care. Teams of two were assigned to rooms and began to see patients. Dave and I set up a "pharmacy" which meant unpacking and organizing the medical supplies we had with us. Pain meds, ointments, bandages, bandaids, cough meds, etc. were sorted so we could quickly provide what was needed. We counted out ten tylenol and put them in little envelopes. We watched as people wept clutching their treasure, knowing that for a few hours they would have relief from pain. Hearing life threatening coughs, seeing wounds not properly treated, watching some struggle to walk using sticks as canes, was more than I could handle at times and I took breaks to pray and get my emotions under control. I felt so ashamed of my lack of appreciation for the expert medical care I enjoyed constantly while these dear people suffered so much. At the end of the day, tired as they were the team told stories of how they had been able to share the love of Jesus through interpreters. Joining hands, the patient's physical and spiritual needs were lifted up in prayer. Our team was "Jesus with skin on" and we felt very privileged to be there.

The next day we found ourselves in a home for the elderly. It was owned by the church and during the day nurses were there to help the residents, serve them meals and provide activities for them.

However, at night the staff had to leave because if they stayed, the government would consider it a medical facility and would move the elderly residents into large government run facilities, lacking the personal loving care provided by the Christian staff. Fortunately, they were just a phone call away if there was an emergency during the night.

Our team members moved from room to room, each with an interpreter, taking blood pressure, temperatures, listening to lungs, changing dressings and tenderly demonstrating the love of Jesus. I went into a room with Sue and while she cared for one woman, her roommate sat on her bed and looked up at me with a big smile. I moved toward her and she reached out and pulled me down to sit by her, all the while clutching my hand. We could not communicate with words but I sensed the hunger in this precious soul for human touch, someone just to be there with her and help pass the long day of boredom. When it was her turn to be examined, she didn't want to let go of my hand but I needed to spend time with her roommate. When Sue finished, we hugged each of them, prayed and with tears streaming down our cheeks, moved to the next room.

That afternoon one of our paramedics had all the residents gather in the dining room. He took a dummy out of a bag, which at first startled them but then laughter erupted as he introduced his pretend patient and through the interpreter, demonstrated how to do CPR. They took turns, wanting to learn so as one of them said, "We can save each other's lives if we can do this." We all laughed when one man said, "I will do mouth to mouth with the ladies!" We did not expect this response from an elderly villager.

After many more hugs, we packed up our equipment and headed home, tired but glad we had been of practical help.

The next morning, in addition to the medical supplies we loaded the boxes of shoes and stuffed lambs in the van. We drove to the local church building where the sanctuary was already packed with parents and children because they had heard we would be giving out shoes. At a glance, we knew there were far more feet than shoes. Dave and I organized the boxes according to shoe sizes and separated boys and girls styles.

I'm not sure how, but the elders of the church controlled the crowd and one by one children came into the room, sat down and allowed us to remove their worn out dirty shoes and replace them with a brand new pair. Sometimes it took more than one try to find the right fit but their eyes lit up and smiles spread across their faces as we handed them their old shoes, hugged them and sent them out with happy hearts and happy feet. Some were wearing flip flops, others bedroom slippers, even though the weather was cold. If a child was hesitant, a parent would hold them on their lap while we fitted the new shoes, all the time expressing their gratitude in Romanian.

As time passed, we had fewer and fewer choices and when the parents realized what was happening, they pushed into the hall in desperation, and the elders had to block the door to our room. It helped that we had cuddly stuffed lambs to place in the arms of those who had no new shoes but our hearts were heavy, knowing that during the winter, in that remote Romanian village, there would be many children with very cold feet.

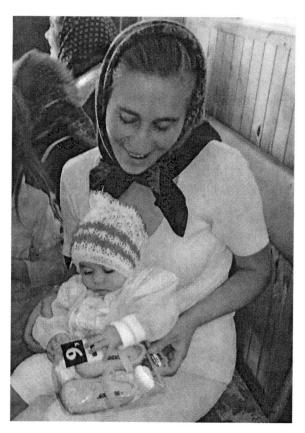

Romanian baby and mother with new shoes

That experience more than any other in my life changed my attitude about "stuff." I have several pairs of shoes, different styles and colors for different occasions, plenty of socks and a closet stuffed with clothes, but I seldom stop to thank my Heavenly Father for His generous provision.

In the closing days of that trip, many tears were shed and prayers offered up as the team met with the church planters to share how God had worked and changed their heart attitudes.

Recently I met Kathy, a nurse who was part of our medical team, in the church foyer. I asked, "Do you ever think about your time in Romania?" She paused for a moment and said, "Yes. I do." "What impressed you most?" She replied, "When we asked the people if we could pray for them, they would shake their heads no and indicate they had no money. Then the translator explained that in the state church, the priest will not pray for someone unless they pay something. We assured them that we just wanted to talk to God on their behalf, so we would hold their hands and pray and when we did, tears streamed down their faces because most of them had never heard their names lifted to God in prayer."

As we drove home I was overwhelmed with a sense of gratitude. God invites us to talk to Him, anytime, anywhere.

'Call to me and I will answer you and tell you great and unsearchable things you do not know' (Jeremiah 33:3, NIV).

There is no payment to be made for this privilege; it is simply a loving Father listening to His child whom He loves with a perfect love.

CHAPTER 12

Some opportunities to serve in Europe touched us more deeply than others but all were meaningful. We were greatly impacted by pastors, missionaries and students alike.

We traveled to Latvia twice to teach English, once in the capital city of Riga and again in a rural setting working with missionaries trying to start a church there. In Riga we taught teens and adults who were interested in improving their English so that they would have greater job opportunities. One day we asked them to talk about their hobbies. Linda brought some of her artwork to show us and wanting to affirm her, I commented about a painting of squash that I thought was particularly well done. The classes went well and when the two weeks were up, we took the bus to the airport to return to Germany.

When we stepped off the bus, there was a group of our students who had come to see us off. They hugged us and gave us small bouquets of flowers to thank us for coming. We sat and chatted over Cokes and when our flight was called, after more hugs Linda handed me a cardboard roll and said, "Don't open this until you get home." I thanked her and was pleasantly surprised when at home I found her gift to be the painting of squash. Not knowing Latvian customs, when someone expresses that they like something that is yours, the polite thing to do is to give it to them. To this day, the painting graces my dining room wall and is a sweet reminder of our students in Riga.

Students from our class met us at
the airport to say goodbye

Years later, we returned to teach English to children in two rural villages. Few of them had any knowledge of English so we played lots of games, taught them simple songs and easy conversations.

In the evening, the church planters played soccer to make friends with folks so, Kally and Jackie, the two teachers with us, joined them to the delight of our young students. Dave and I joined the cheering section. Our being there helped greatly in building positive relationships.

North of Latvia is Estonia, another Baltic state. We took teams to teach English eight times, and felt very much at home there. The churches were warm and welcoming and the people genuine in their desire to learn English. The church in Kehra purchased a government building when the communists left and remodeled it. The lunch room became the sanctuary, the offices were changed into bedrooms for visitors and at each end of the second floor hallway, were apartments for the pastor and assistant pastor. One year we were able to teach in two locations, so we took a team of 18 people. One shower for all of us was quite a challenge but having a sign-up sheet helped.

The Estonians loved to show us some of the sights including an ancient monastery, castles, a cranberry bog, a view of Russia and a chance to freeze our feet in the North Sea. We were also invited for meals in many of their homes including the pastor's. His wife had a lovely teapot, painted with flowers. Joyce exclaimed over its beauty and before we left, she found it wrapped as a gift for her to take home. We had failed to realize that Estonians were the same as Latvians in their generosity toward those who compliment something. For Joyce, it is a treasured reminder of her students and teaching experience there.

Our students were especially excited the year that we used teaching material based on the Narnia movie. They heard it in English with subtitles in Estonian. The men of the church built a wardrobe in the hall by one entrance, so each night, they were able to walk through it in order to get to Narnia, our meeting room. The teachers wore shirts showing a picture of Aslan. We had some extras that we gave as awards and one student, who worked as a cashier at the grocery store, desperately wanted a shirt. She didn't win one but our last night there, I washed Dave's shirt and the next morning we took it to her. Delighted she ran around the counter and gave us big hugs.

One year a team worked on the church property, while we taught English classes. They built a very large sandbox under a huge willow tree in the front yard. We thought it was a strange project but actually, it was a wonderful idea. Moms from all over town brought their children there to play and women from the church built relationships that led to a Bible study and opportunities to teach the young children about Jesus.

Relationships were built as mothers brought
their children to play in the sand

Many people gave up two weeks of their vacations to go with us. Friendships still continue through email and the church has grown, encouraging those believers.

France was our destination several times during our seven years in Europe. After moving back to the U.S., we continued to take teams each summer. We felt quite at home in Paris, teaching English in a church on the outskirts of the city. The students were more cosmopolitan, yet French through and through. Many had a good background in English and wanted to improve their pronunciation and practice by talking with native English speakers. Of all the countries we visited, they were the most resistant to spiritual truth but the missionaries were encouraged when some students came to small conversation groups that they offered after the two weeks of classes ended.

New Year's Eve in France was a unique experience for us. A church heard of my black light chalk drawings and invited us to come and be a part of their celebration. As I drew, a friend fluent in French, read my devotional. At the conclusion, I turned on the black light to reveal a hidden picture of Christ with His hands outspread inviting them to follow Him throughout the new year. After praying, the lights came on and since it was almost midnight everyone went outside. Within moments fireworks began and the celebration was in full swing. Wine and cheese, pastries of all kinds and other delicacies were served. Traditional dances were performed and we realized this was going to be an all night event. We had a long drive ahead of us, so after awhile, headed back to Germany our heads full of wonderful memories of New Year's Eve...French style.

Portugal was an easy drive from where we lived so at the invitation of missionary friends there, we loaded my equipment into our hatchback and headed out to celebrate the 25th Anniversary of the Portuguese Bible Institute. We were thrilled to see how the school had grown and faithfully prepared young people to serve the Lord. Their school choir sang as I drew and then I shared a message challenging them to be faithful to God's call.

Micki drawing while the PBI choir sang

On Sunday we enjoyed the enthusiasm of the local church service, delicious food and conversation with those who spoke English. As we drove back home, we rejoiced in another opportunity to see how God was building His church throughout Europe.

Not many people have an opportunity like this. "How about joining our team in Torino, Italy to do outreach during the Olympic Games?" "This is way out of our comfort zone but can I use my blacklight drawing there?" I asked. "Sure. You can draw while the rock group that we are taking plays." The plan was that the group would play out on the plaza during the day and when a crowd gathered to listen to them, we would pass out invitations to a concert to be held at night, in the nearby storefront church. We walked around after the band played and tried to engage people in conversation if they spoke English. The goal was to share Christ and offer them literature about the church and what it means to be a follower of Christ. Over and over I prayed and walked toward a person only, to be ignored or waved away. I hated being rejected and wanted to just quit but the rest of the team were talking to people, so I needed to keep trying and hope for the best. Eventually it was time for supper and to prepare for the concert and my time to draw. The band could be heard outside which drew people in and it wasn't long before the room was full. I began my drawing of Christ on the cross and when complete, the lights were turned off and the black light turned on revealing the risen Savior. In Italian, the people were invited to place their faith in Jesus. After a prayer, the lights came on again and the music blasted to the delight of the crowd. I'm not a fan of rock music but must admit this group was good!

One of the team members had a relative competing in the games so the next night we were able to attend a session of speed skating preliminaries. Being in the stadium, feeling the excitement and watching these athletes who had trained for years compete, was awe inspiring. If that wasn't enough, after the event, we were able to attend a party for the speed skating team. When we arrived the skater said, "I'm here with twenty of my friends. May we come in?" "Sure," they said and so we ate snacks and talked with the competitors.

God opened many different doors for us and our lives were enriched by each experience.

Even though years have passed, people and places still fill our minds and at dinner, we rehearse what God did both in and through us during our years in Europe.

CHAPTER 13

I'm seated at the computer unsure as to how to start this chapter. Perhaps it is because it is extremely important to me that I communicate what is on my heart. Since early childhood, talking with God has been a lifeline for me. That line winds its way through each chapter of my life becoming stronger with each passing year.

> "In the morning, O Lord, you hear my voice; in the morning I lay my requests before you and wait in expectation" (Psalm 5:3, NIV).

I wake with the sweet consciousness of His presence, knowing He does not sleep and is with me through the night. How can I help but praise Him and confess any known sin so that He is not grieved. I pause to put on the armor He provides.

The Helmet of Salvation to guard my mind and guide my thoughts
The Breastplate of Righteousness to guard my heart and emotions
The Belt of Truth to protect me from Satan's lies
The Shoes of Peace enabling me to share the Gospel
The Shield of Faith to protect from the enemy
The Sword of the Spirit, which is the Word of God to fight against the enemy

Then with thanksgiving, I make my requests and move into my day with expectation of what He will do and how He will guide me. There need not be constant conversation but still there is communication and I can use my words to talk to Him at any time just as his Spirit speaks quietly in my inner being. When I need wisdom, all I have to do is ask and it is given liberally. When my faith wavers, He often takes me back to times when it was tested and He proved faithful.

My son Jerry was a pilot in the Air Force, stationed at Sheppard Air Force Base. He was flying T-38's training other pilots. I had seen God work in his life to prepare him for a military career. He graduated from the Air Force Academy and was fulfilling his dream of being a pilot. To fly F-16 fighter jets was his ultimate goal. I really struggled. I knew God had opened this door for him. I knew he was a child of God and I knew that God was always with him but still fear often crept into my mind knowing he was out there in the "wild blue yonder". One night the phone rang and it was Becky, his wife.

"Just in case it's on the news tonight, I thought I better let you know that Jerry had to eject from his plane before it crashed tonight. He and his student from Germany are shaken up but have no serious injuries." She went on to explain that they were doing an exercise to practice landings where they touch down and take off immediately. As they were doing the last go around, they flew through a flock of birds, stalling both engines. When every procedure to restart them failed, Jerry gave the command to his student to eject and in seconds his canopy flew off and he was out. As best he could, he set the plane's course away from populated areas. Jerry pushed the button and his canopy disappeared and he too, was ejected. After consciousness returned, Jerry sensed that his chute was open and spotted the other pilot, below him. He waited to hear the crash of the plane but there was only silence. They landed in a field behind some houses and people called Becky to let her know Jerry was okay and 911 to take them to the hospital to be checked. They still didn't know what happened to the plane.

After some time word came. The pilotless plane had glided down, sheared the wheat in a field, crossed a highway between two utility poles, under the power lines and came to a stop in a grassy area in front of a factory. It didn't crash! One TV commentator said, "Now that's real luck." He didn't realize that there was a pilot though not visible to human eyes and I wept as I later watched the recorded newscast concerning the flight. I felt God said to me, "Micki, now can you trust me with your son? I'm holding his life in my loving hands. There is no reason to fear, my child." Logically you would think that after that incident I would have worried more but the opposite was true. Having seen how God miraculously intervened, since that time I have been able to trust more fully and know that He has everything under control.

Years later, in Germany I went through a time of despair. The phone rang in the middle of the night. "Mom, I don't want to go on living," my daughter said. I was stunned. I knew she had struggled with depression but had no idea it was so serious. Trying to gather my thoughts, we talked and I listened as she shared her feelings. We knew when we left for Germany it would be challenging but I also knew that only God could deliver her. In a note to us before we left she said, "These are going to be the hardest years of my life." That seemed to be true as we talked and I prayed with her that night. Eventually, when I sensed she was not suicidal, our conversation ended. I slept little and cried much through the rest of the night. I prayed, but there was no peace. I read scripture, but found no answers. In the days that followed friends expressed concern for me. Finally, one day a friend came with two German friends from her church. "We have come to pray with you. Satan is on the attack and you need to be delivered from this depression and so does your daughter." They gathered around me as I sat in a chair, one kneeling in front of me, the other two lovingly holding my hands and took turns praying. They praised God for Christ's victory over Satan at the cross. They rebuked Satan and prayed at length for victory in my life and the life of my daughter. As they did, I felt the despair melt away and hope filled my heart. A renewed sense of Christ's presence surrounded me and I was delivered from the enemy. We praised God together filled with much joy. Not long after that the phone rang again and it was my daughter. "Mom," she said, "That awful depression that has been surrounding me is gone! I can't believe it." I told her what had happened for me as well. That was not the end of her struggle but at least for that time in her life, God intervened and protected her from the enemy. Our adversary wants to destroy but Christ has overcome him and prayer and the word of God are our weapons against him.

One of these friends attended a Disciple's Prayer Life study group. When she invited me to join I knew that was exactly what I needed. Prayer had always been an important part of my life but I longed for more. In one of the sessions, the leader invited us to sit quietly in God's presence and ask the Spirit to reveal any sin in our hearts. Everyone was quiet and before long, tears started running down my cheeks. I didn't understand at first, but soon the Spirit said to me, "What are those stones in your lap?" I hadn't been aware of them but suddenly felt the terrible weight. There they were. Envy. Jealousy. Anger. A critical spirit. Judging others. There was the pile and deep inside I wanted to throw them at others but heard Jesus' words to the crowd, "He that is without sin, let him cast the first stone." Tearfully in my mind, I laid each stone at Jesus' feet and asked for forgiveness. I realized that day how easy it is to judge others and how hard it is to keep oneself pure. Several others had been touched as well, so we shared what God had taught us and prayed for one another. That was many years ago, but what I learned that day is still real and relevant.

We are often reminded of how vital prayer was when we took teams of people to teach English. One woman took it upon herself to follow the pastor around and point out to him all the things he should be doing "like we do in America." He worked full-time to support his family as well as pastoring the church, so the ministry was effective though somewhat limited. When we saw what she was doing, after much prayer, we met with her and explained that her behavior and attitude were totally unacceptable and if she was not able to change, we would have to send her home. As we prayed with her, she repented and God used her throughout the rest of her time there.

Then there was the team member who went off on his own and so we stood on the street corner praying that God would direct his steps back to the group so that he wouldn't miss the only train back to the church that day. In addition to lost people, we had a lost computer. Somehow it was left on the train platform, but after much prayer and a long train ride back to the station, with the help of a missionary we were able to convince the French authorities that it was ours.

Recently God taught me something else. While visiting our daughter, we went to the grocery store with her and her two children. Later that evening, having put away the groceries, eaten dinner and tucked the children into bed, the search began for her cell phone. It was her only means of communication, contained important information and was a vital part of her life as a single mom. After searching the house and car, she tearfully collapsed on her bed exhausted. I offered to go to the store and see if anyone had turned it in, so her dad and I began our quest. When we arrived at the parking lot, I got out of the car, raised my hands to heaven and prayed, "Father, you are the great I AM, creator of the universe and it's hard for me to believe that You care about a cell phone, but I ask, in Jesus name and to show my daughter your great love, that you help us find the phone."

We began by looking in all the carts scattered in the lot. No phone. We went in and asked at the service desk if it had been turned in. No phone. Our only hope now was to walk along the rows of empty carts lined up outside the store and to use our phone to call her number and see if we heard anything. We started with the carts to the left of the doors but we heard nothing. Then we moved to the carts to the right of the door. I dialed her number as we walked along and suddenly, I heard her phone. I could hardly believe it! We located the sound and of course it was in the middle of three long lines of carts which meant we had to move a lot of them to reach it. After much effort, we found it on the ground in the row closest to the wall, picked it up and immediately praised God. In all of His greatness, He cares about the little things. At home, I raced up the stairs, knelt by my daughter's bed and as I handed her the phone said, "Don't you EVER doubt God's love for you." Before going to sleep we shared hugs and more prayers of thanksgiving. I'm sure there is no end to what God will teach me of my lifeline to Him, through prayer especially as I move into the last chapter of my life.

CHAPTER 14

Through the years, our travels have taken us to forty-seven states in the U.S., Canada, Mexico and thirty-three countries in Europe. Moonlit valleys, Mirror Lake and spectacular waterfalls in Yosemite National Park, the Teton Mountains range, Yellowstone National Park in Wyoming and the Grand Canyon are favorites out west. In the east, Niagara Falls is unmatched in its awesome power and majesty. Turquoise waters lapping pristine white sand beaches and the spectacular underwater world of coral reefs, in the Caribbean and Hawaii display the splendor of God's creation.

Two other beautiful places are my favorites, one in Croatia and the other in Switzerland. Plitvice Lakes National Park is in Croatia. Tucked away in this forest covered landscape are sixteen blue and green lakes, large and small, each one at a lower level than the next. They are linked with foaming cascades and pounding waterfalls, created by water from little brooks and streams. Walkways allowed us to wander through, drinking in the beauty and watching the fish through the crystal clear water. Some places are hard to describe in words, this being one of them. My other favorite is a walking path in the Swiss Alps. A cable car took us high up above the valley. A winding path led through forests and meadows, where tinkling cowbells and abundant wildflowers added to the charm of our surroundings. All the while, we gazed across at three snowcapped peaks, reaching majestically toward heaven. Some visitors, who joined us on this walk, spontaneously sang the Doxology, moved by the beauty. I long to have sights such as these as part of the new earth that we will enjoy for eternity. Unfortunately, our days of such travels have ended. Now I need to fix my eyes on what God is preparing for me in the future.

> "No eye has seen, no ear has heard, no mind has conceived what God has prepared for those who love him" (1 Corinthians 2:9, NIV).

What I have seen and experienced has been wonderful but what awaits me now?

Paul writes, "Though outwardly we are wasting away, yet inwardly we are being renewed day by day. For our light and momentary troubles are achieving for us an eternal glory that far outweighs them all. So we fix our eyes not on what is seen, but what is unseen. For what is seen is temporary, but what is unseen is eternal" (2 Corinthians 4: 16-18, NIV).

I have enjoyed excellent health most of my life, troubled only by an irritating cough from time to time and some bouts of pneumonia and bronchitis. Two years ago, I went to my pulmonary doctor for a check-up. I was alarmed when he said, "I want you to see one of my associates for further evaluation. Before you leave today, schedule an appointment. Here is an order for a CT scan of your lungs." Weeks later when the scan results were in, I met with Dr. Pantano for the first time. After listening to my lungs and viewing the test results, he said, "I don't like to have to tell you this but you have Idiopathic Pulmonary Fibrosis. Idiopathic means we don't know the cause and as of today there is no cure. The good news is, if you are willing I can put you on an experimental drug that slows the progress of the disease. Why don't you think about it and if you are interested, meet with my associate who handles the drug program."

I drove home in a state of shock. I wasn't at all prepared for this. I had never smoked, had exercised, had eaten right and did all the T.V. commercials say to do to be "healthy, wealthy and wise." Now this. Through my tears I said, "Why me, God?" I was angry and scared and heard no answer. When I shared my diagnosis with Dave, he was understanding and comforted me as best he could.

The next morning I turned to Psalm 34 (NIV) that I had chosen to focus on that year.

"The eyes of the Lord are on the righteous and his ears attentive to their cry (v 15),

The righteous cry out, and the Lord hears them; he delivers them from all their troubles.

The Lord is close to the brokenhearted and saves those who are crushed in spirit." (v 17-18).

That was a picture of me. The night before, the noise of my fussing, drowned out His still small voice but in the morning, I could hear Him. I went on to read, "I sought the Lord, and he answered me; he delivered me from all my fears" (Psalm 34: 4, NIV).

As Dave and I ate breakfast and talked, we both felt we should take advantage of the experimental drug being offered. I made the appointment and in a few weeks was approved to take the medication. Of course there were risks and long lists of side effects but I could go off of it at any time.

I received my first bottle of pills through the mail. I had shared my diagnosis with family and a few friends and together we prayed that I could tolerate the drug without severe side effects. At first, things went well but as weeks passed I had difficulty eating and my weight began to drop. I had little energy and slept often during the day. Joint pain troubled me and my skin itched for no reason. I found myself obsessed with death. I would walk by a painting on the wall and think, "Who should I leave that to when I die?" It took very little to trigger the tears that were always ready to spill down my cheeks. We decided to get a second opinion and took the train to Northwestern University Hospital in downtown Chicago. I was greatly impressed with how efficient they were, spending a great deal of time reviewing my history and suggesting a plan. Dr. Lamm was compassionate and very knowledgeable of my disease. She said that once a month a group of doctors met and reviewed cases such as mine. She ordered tests to find out if there was possibly some other cause. Weeks later we met with her again and she shared their findings. "All of the doctors reviewed your test results and we agree that you do have IPF. There is another drug I use with my patients if they can't tolerate the one you are on, so talk to your doctor about that possibility," she said. My heart sank as we made our way home. I had hoped that she would not confirm my diagnosis.

The next morning at my Bible Study group at church, they asked me what had happened at the appointment. Tears came and unable to answer, a friend escorted me to the prayer chapel where I sobbed uncontrollably. She went and asked Pastor Andrew to come. He came and sat down by me, his strong arm around my shoulders. "I don't want this," I cried. "I don't want it for you either," he said. I felt guilty for feeling that way but he comforted me and told me it was okay to cry and grieve the loss of health, the impact of the disease and the realization that it was terminal. After talking and praying, my emotions calmed and he went with me to the Bible study group. He explained the situation and said, "As the body of Christ, we will walk with Micki through this, giving her the love and support she needs" and that has been a beautiful reality since that day.

I was blessed to have a healthy husband and assumed that he would be there to take care of me. He had jogged for more than thirty years so I was a shocked one Saturday morning, when the doorbell rang and a woman asked, "Is that your husband?" She pointed to Dave as he lay on the sidewalk, in front of our house. Seeing that he was unable to get up, I dialed 911 and could barely get the words out as my heart pounded and breath failed. The paramedics came quickly, got him into the ambulance along with me and my oxygen tank. Dave didn't know what caused him to fall and had quite a black eye and facial abrasions from hitting his head. X-rays showed no concussion so they sent him home. He seemed somewhat unsteady on his feet but we thought it was just fear of falling again.

Two weeks later as we ate lunch together, I sensed something was wrong. He was unable to talk and although it was only momentary, it was frightening. He agreed to go to see a doctor on Monday. More tests were ordered and the following Sunday he had significant trouble expressing himself. Fearing a stroke, it was off to the hospital, this time to be admitted. Within an hour an IV of an anti-seizure drug was introduced and he returned to normal. The scan they took showed blood between the skull and the brain which probably was a result of the fall weeks earlier. Home again, we rejoiced that it was resolved and began planning a trip to Arizona to spend Christmas with family.

We flew to Arizona and a few days before Christmas, our daughter was going to a clinic because of a cough. Dave decided to go along, having had a urinary problem during the night. That turned out to be nothing important but the nurse observed that his foot was swollen, did an ultrasound and said, "You need to go directly to the hospital. This is a life-threatening situation." I thought, "God. What's going on? We came here to relax and enjoy Christmas with family, not deal with more illness." Tests showed blood clots in his leg and lung, so we spent Christmas in the hospital for the first time in our marriage. A sense of calm came over me, as I realized that we were surrounded with those who loved us and would be there for us in this time of need. I was able to be a part of the family celebration and watched as my two grandsons and their wives, took great delight in their five little boys tearing open packages and shouting with glee. Jerry and Becky love their role as grandparents and bought gifts they knew their little grandsons would love.

My daughter Cheryl and her two children came to the hospital on Christmas Eve with a blanket and food so we could "picnic" in Grampa's room. It was a far cry from our traditional Christmas Eve, but is a fun memory. After all, we were together, celebrating Jesus' birth. Isn't that what Christmas should be all about? When visitor's hours ended, I sadly kissed Dave goodbye. I was exhausted but couldn't resist getting ready for bed, packing what I needed for the morning and driving to Cheryl's to spend the night. After all, I needed to be there to read Keaira and Anglas Christmas books, see them hang up their stockings and leave cookies for Santa. I slept on the couch until two very excited children decided it was time to be up. More tearing open of gifts, playing with toys and treasuring up memories filled the time until I left to spend Christmas with Dave in the hospital. I couldn't understand why, at a time when I needed to be cared for, I was thrust into the role of caretaker but God's strength was sufficient for each day.

Back home, Dave couldn't drive for six months because of the seizures so that was my job. One day he wanted me to go to the bank and for some reason I got angry. I didn't want to go out, much less to do banking which he normally did, but he insisted. I didn't bother to take oxygen, so I was somewhat out of breath when I got to the bank. I stood in the queue, breathing hard until a teller motioned for me to come. I leaned on the counter and explained that my husband usually did the withdrawals but that he was not well, so I had to come. She looked at me and said "Well, you are beautiful, inside and out," then turned to do what I had requested. I was stunned. What prompted her to say such a thing? When she returned I said, "If you see any beauty in me, it's because I am a Christ follower and His Spirit lives in me." She reached for my hand and said, "I am a believer, too and I am going to pray for you and your husband." Rather than scold me, my loving Father used her kind words to affirm me and I left the bank amazed at His goodness.

> "For God, who said, 'Let light shine out of darkness,' made his light shine in our hearts to give us the light of the knowledge of the glory of God in the face of Christ. But we have this treasure in jars of clay to show that this all-surpassing power is from God and not from us. We are hard pressed on every side, but not crushed; perplexed, but not in despair" (2 Corinthians 4:6-8, NIV).

Being on a new drug, I have fewer side effects. Although I have lost half of my lung function and use oxygen most of the time, I no longer focus on death even though I dread the path I must travel with this illness. After all, we are all terminal and only God knows when and how our time on earth will end. As I live day by day, I do however think often of heaven. What does it mean that Christ is preparing a dwelling place for me? What will I do forever and ever and ever? I am thankful that there will be no more tears, no more pain and no more shortness of breath. Instead, beauty beyond anything my eyes have ever seen will surround me and most importantly, I will see Jesus face to face.

Then, there is the anticipated separation that I can't even think about. Only by the grace which God has promised, only as I walk with my hand in His, will I be able to say goodbye to those I love so dearly.

An email message from Alin, the young man who trusted Christ while I was at camp in Romania says, "May God bless you and encourage you every day, and be confident in the hope that we received from our Jesus Christ, through His Holy Spirit and His Holy Word. It's such a wonderful feeling knowing that this life is not all and in a blessed day, all of us who believe in His sacrifice and now are doing His will, will be taken in His Glory and will spend all the eternity in His presence."

And to that I say, Amen.

A NOTE FROM THE AUTHOR

Healing
It comes without warning by day or by night
    beyond all description
    dispelling all light.

Its fingers clutch tightly the hearts of those near
    the lifebreath is stifled
    and tear follows tear.

Although one can see it and quick is its work
    the heart is unwilling
    and dim hopes still lurk.

To whom can the heart turn, when broken it lies
    in anguish unbearable
    softly it cries.

The answer comes not but time takes its flight
    and with it comes healing
    and slowly the light.

Beyond explanation this healing of time
    yet great is its mission
    to all of mankind.

Micki Green

CPSIA information can be obtained
at www.ICGtesting.com
Printed in the USA
FFOW02n0849011116
28935FF